D1524474

What's this weird but cute animal?

It's an **orchid mantis.**

Contents

Credits

Cover, © Sebastian Janicki/Shutterstock; TOC, © Eric Isselee/Shutterstock; 4–5, © Chien Lee/Minden Pictures; 6L, © seeyou/Shutterstock; 6–7, © Vince Adam/Shutterstock; 8, © SHAWSHANK61/iStock; 9T, © Ivoha/Shutterstock; 9B, © Kurit afshen/Shutterstock; 10L, © Dwight Kuhn; 10R, © irin-k/Shutterstock; 11, © Dwight Kuhn; 12, © Dwight Kuhn; 13, © Francesco Tomasinelli/Science Source; 14L, © FLPA/Alamy; 14–15, © Unno Kazuo/Nature Production/Minden Pictures; 16T, © Chien Lee/Minden Pictures; 16B, © Chien Lee/Minden Pictures; 17, © Luc Viatour/CC BY-SA 4.0; 18L, © Vince Adam/Shutterstock; 18R, © Eric Isselee/Shutterstock; 19T, © Koji Yamazaki/Nature Production; 19B, © Diana Meister/Alamy; 20L, © Antonio Guillem/Shutterstock and © Andrey Lobachev/Shutterstock; 20–21, © Koji Yamazaki/Nature Production/Minden Pictures; 22 (T to B), © Viktor Loki/Shutterstock, © WILDLIFE GmbH/Alamy, and © fntproject/Shutterstock; 23TL, © Savushkin/iStock; 23TR, © Dwight Kuhn; 23BL, © Dwight Kuhn; 23BR, © FLPA/Alamy.

Publisher: Kenn Goin
Senior Editor: Joyce Tavolacci
Creative Director: Spencer Brinker
Design: Debrah Kaiser
Photo Researcher: Thomas Persano

Library of Congress Cataloging-in-Publication Data

Names: Merwin, E., author.
Title: Orchid mantis / by E. Merwin.
Description: New York, New York : Bearport Publishing, 2018. | Series: Even weirder and cuter | Includes bibliographical references and index.
Identifiers: LCCN 2017045549 (print) | LCCN 2017045814 (ebook) | ISBN 9781684025206 (ebook) | ISBN 9781684024629 (library)
Subjects: LCSH: Orchid mantis—Juvenile literature.
Classification: LCC QL505.9.H94 (ebook) | LCC QL505.9.H94 M47 2018 (print) | DDC 595.7/27—dc23
LC record available at https://lccn.loc.gov/2017045549

For more information, write to Bearport Publishing Company, Inc., 45 West 21st Street, Suite 3B, New York, New York 10010. Printed in the United States of America.

10 9 8 7 6 5 4 3 2 1

Orchid Mantis

by E. Merwin

Consultant: Darin Collins, DVM
Director, Animal Health Programs
Woodland Park Zoo
Seattle, Washington

BEARPORT
PUBLISHING

New York, New York

Big, bulging **eye**s!

Spiny front legs!

Is that a blossom or a bug?

The female orchid mantis looks just like a flower!

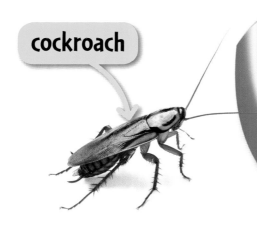

cockroach

An orchid mantis is a kind of **insect**. It's related to a cockroach.

6

orchid mantis

flower

7

The orchid mantis perches on a stem.

She rocks on her petal-like legs.

She **mimics** a flower blowing in the breeze!

These insects live in rain forests in Southeast Asia.

9

Bees and other bugs are drawn to the fake flower.

They are doomed to be dinner!

The mantis snatches up her **prey** with her front legs.

bee

A mantis's front legs have sharp spines. The spines help the insect catch and hold prey.

Now the mantis chomps down.

She eats her prey alive—
and head first!

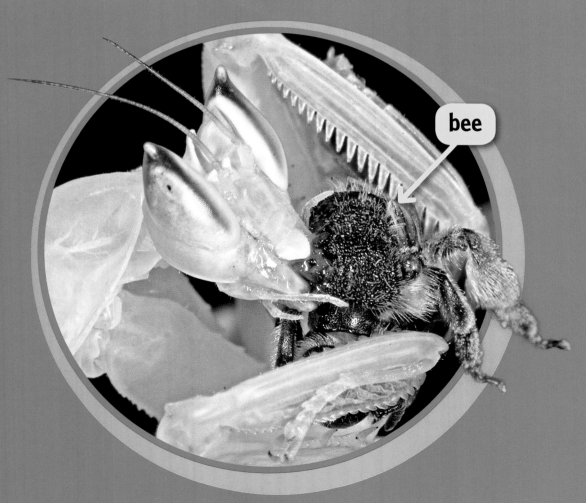

bee

orchid mantis

butterfly

An orchid mantis eats mostly insects, including butterflies.

The orchid mantis has enemies, too.

Her flowery body helps her hide.

Predators often don't see her!

gecko

The mantis's enemies include lizards, spiders, and snakes.

15

Watch out!

The orchid mantis keeps an eye out for enemies.

She can turn her head 180 degrees.

That's a full half circle!

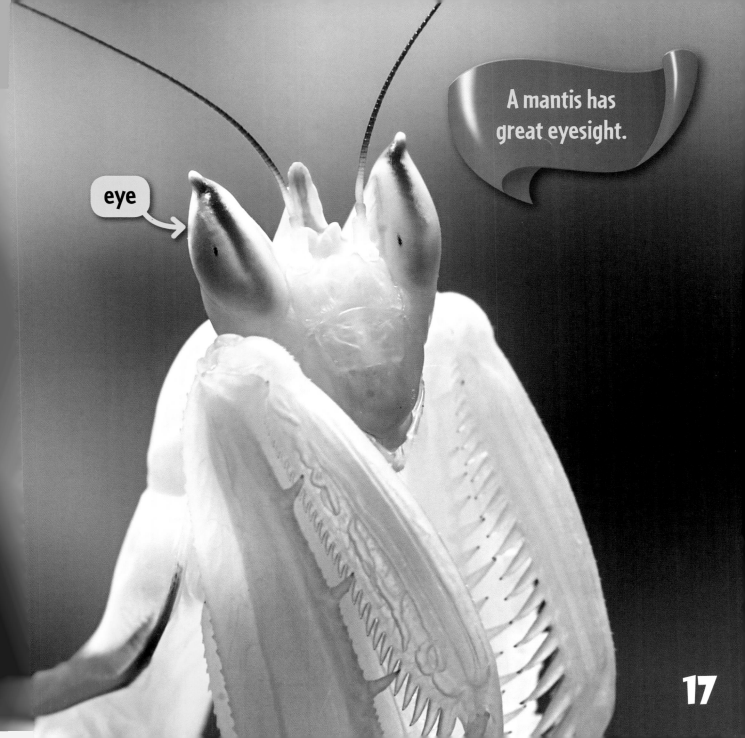

17

The female mantis has a special way of laying eggs.

She covers them with a bubbly foam.

The foam hardens into a long egg sack.

egg sack

The babies hatch a few weeks later.

female mantis

Baby orchid mantises also fool enemies. They look like bad-tasting assassin (uh-SASS-in) bugs.

baby orchid mantis

baby assassin bug

A female orchid mantis grows to be as long as a human thumb.

The male is tiny— only about the size of a quarter.

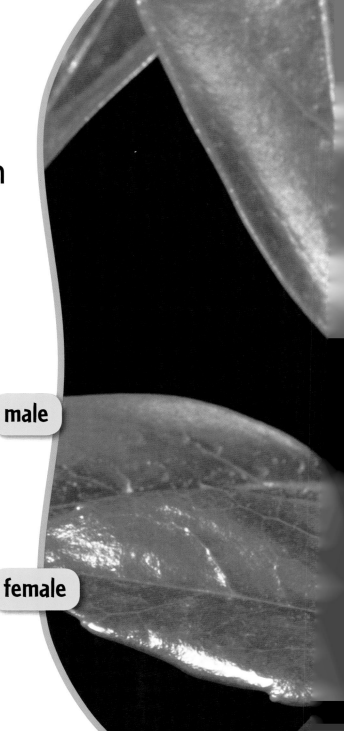

male

female

The male must beware.

A hungry female might eat him, too!

male

female

The small male mantis is often less colorful than the female.

More Weird Mantises

Conehead Mantis
This mantis lives in Europe. It looks like a dead twig—or, some might say, an alien! It has a long, thin body and a pointed head.

Devil's Flower Mantis
When under attack, this large African mantis spreads out its front legs. By doing this, the insect appears even bigger!

Peruvian Shield Mantis
This mantis has a big, green shield on its neck. Its body shape and green color help it hide among leaves in forests.

Glossary

insect (IN-sekt) an animal that has six legs, three main body parts, two antennas, and a hard covering called an exoskeleton

mimics (MIM-iks) resembles another thing, such as a flower

predators (PRED-uh-turz) animals that hunt other animals for food

prey (PRAY) an animal that is hunted and eaten by another animal

Index

Read More

Gleason, Carrie. *Everything Insects: All the Facts, Photos, and Fun to Make You Buzz!* Washington, DC: National Geographic (2015).

Honovich, Nancy, and Darlyne Murawski. *Ultimate Bugopedia: The Most Complete Bug Reference Ever.* Washington, DC: National Geographic (2013).

Learn More Online

To learn more about orchid mantises, visit
www.bearportpublishing.com/EvenWeirderAndCuter

About the Author

E. Merwin is honored to share planet Earth with
10 quintillion (10,000,000,000,000,000,000) insects—
give or take a few!